Breaking Free:

12 Steps to Sexual Purity for Men

Stephen Wood

Family Life Center Publications

ISBN: 0-9727571-1-2
Library of Congress Control Number: 2003109711
Book production: Family Life Center Publications
Cover & layout design: Catherine Wood
Manufactured in the United States of America

Acknowledgments

I would like to thank my wife Karen and my daughter Stephanie
for their proofreading. I also thank my daughter Catherine for
the cover design and text layout. I express special gratitude to
Philip Cutajar for his proofreading and editing.

Family Life Center Publications
22226 Westchester Blvd.
Port Charlotte, FL 33952
www.familylifecenter.net

Contents

FOREWORD

Screwtape's Strategies to Destroy Family Life

The Screwtape Letters, a book by C.S. Lewis, unveils a series of secret correspondence between a senior demon, Screwtape, and his neophyte tempter and nephew Wormwood. Lewis uses a type of reverse theology to warn Christians against diabolical temptation strategies. The following account illustrates how Screwtape might advise utilizing the darker sides of the Internet to ensnare Christian men.

Screwtape's Strategies to Destroy Family Life

My Dear Wormwood:

For your careful review, I have outlined below our strategies for destroying the Faith and family life. Destroy this secret message immediately after reading it. This classified material comes from the lowest regions.

In this new millennium, we must use technology to bring our master plan to completion by utilizing Internet pornography. Already we have spiritually neutralized millions of the Enemy's men with pornography. Over the next few years we can surely make millions more spiritual midgets, whom we can then manipulate at will.

It is so encouraging that Internet pornography has ensnared so many millions of Christian men. These fools think there is no harm in a few clicks to dirty Web sites. Little do they know that we can't wait to use their growing porn addiction to drive a wedge between them and their despicable brides.

You see, the delightful byproduct of pornography addiction is that it is so effective in creating turmoil in marriages. Of course, we have been attempting to destroy marriages as a vital part of our overall plan. A husband's pornography addiction has shown a unique ability to undermine trust and intimacy between spouses. The addiction creates turmoil, heartbreak, and bewilderment in the hearts of those detestable Christian wives. It's so amusing to watch marriages fall apart when husbands assume that their wives actually believe their deceptions and lies about not having a porn addiction.

With Internet pornography we can finally bring down the guardians of the Christian family. The fools still don't realize that the technological temptations are waging war against their very souls, bringing to completion a more-than-a-century-long campaign to destroy the Faith by destroying the family. Since it is working so exceedingly well, I suggest that we continue to use every technological innovation to pump pornography to Christian men. Just think of the wonderful new digital temptations we are sending out over broadband!

Remember, every man addicted to pornography is caught in the snares of what the Enemy calls grave sin. With pornography we have crippled their ability to spiritually protect themselves and their families. After they are ensnared in pornography, their families (their marriages and their children) are vulnerable to our attacks. Sure, these men still appear fine on the outside as they go to church, but we know that their hearts have been captured by pornography.

And since sons usually follow in their father's footsteps, the sins of the fathers will run down through the generations, and we can rest assured that the future generations will belong to us.

As far as Sundays in church go, there is only one thing to do. Just make sure things stay as they are— nice and quiet. The last thing we need are homilies about specific sins such as pornography. If a damaging homily is somehow preached, make sure you scramble any attempts to organize support groups to assist men unable to free themselves from our work. Just let the poor devils struggle alone— though of course we know that they are not alone in their pornography addiction, don't we?

Finally, we must keep up our guard against the Head of THAT family. Never forget how the Head of THAT family was used by the Enemy to ruin our dear servant Herod's plans to kill the so-called Holy One. There are centuries-old rumors from the upper regions that the Head of THAT family will be brought into service at a critical time in history. The last thing we want is a repeat of the first century.

It has taken immense effort, but we have managed thoroughly to confuse modern man (and much of the Church) about the meaning of true manhood and masculinity. We need impure men, especially husbands and fathers, to continue leading the culture towards our regions. We must therefore keep men from contact with the Head of THAT family, so that they don't have any effective models of manly purity and righteousness.

Yet we need to be realistic in our strategies. If we

cannot keep men away from the Unmentionable One, then at least we can chip away at some of the truth to keep things manageable for us. Keep their beliefs abstract. Men look up to tangible role models. Just be sure they don't discover the Enemy's perfect model for husbands and fathers, or our plans will get derailed. We can never hope to lead fathers who are devoted to that so-called "Just Man" deeper into the depraved delights of pornography.

Yours diabolically,

Screwtape

12 Steps to Sexual Purity

Here are twelve important steps which, if all are followed, should greatly assist you in breaking your addiction:

STEP

1

Destroy All of Your Pornography

Destroy all pornographic magazines, photographs, videos, CDs, and all pornographic Internet bookmarks and files on your computer. Do it right now! You can't "just sort of" want purity and expect to obtain it. You have to make a heartfelt decision to break free of pornography, and then act upon that decision.

Temptations for men usually come through the eye. Jesus advocates radical steps to rid our lives of anything we look at that would cause us to sin.

"If your right eye causes you to sin, pluck it out and throw it away; it is better that you lose one of your members than that your whole body be thrown into hell." - Matthew 5:29

STEP

2

Take Radical Steps to Re-orient Your Life

The Catechism says, "Sexuality affects all aspects of the human person" (Section 2332). Therefore, if you are under the influence of a life-dominating sexual sin like pornography addiction, you need to take radical steps to re-orient your life. You must develop a protection plan in order to avoid both the remote and the proximate occasions of sin. This may mean: shopping at different stores to avoid even glancing at pornography; taking a different route home; breaking with any routine likely to result in sin; carrying small amounts of cash; canceling subscriptions to newspapers containing lingerie ads and inserts; canceling certain cable channels – or getting rid of cable altogether; and/or stopping channel surfing. Take these steps now!

"Let us then cast off the works of darkness and put on the armor of light; let us conduct ourselves becomingly as in the day, not in reveling and drunkenness, not in debauchery and licentiousness, not in quarreling and jealousy. But put on the Lord Jesus Christ, and make no provision for the flesh, to gratify its desires." - Romans 13:12-14

(Note: St. Augustine once turned to this passage at random. Reading it prompted a radical conversion and a turning from his licentious lifestyle.)

For the Internet you need to either install a good filtering program where your wife or a good friend holds the passwords, or subscribe to a "clean" Internet provider. You also need to move your home computer to an open location in the home. Similar steps must be taken with your workplace computer; *The Industry Standard* has reported that 70% of Internet porn traffic occurs between 9 a.m. and 5 p.m. (cited in the *National Catholic Register*, 6/19/00).

Find a Priest to Work With You

Try to find a priest experienced in helping men overcome pornography addictions. Make frequent use of the Sacrament of Penance. Be honest and forthcoming. Remember, a priest cannot prescribe a cure unless he has all the facts in hand.

I have encountered Catholic men addicted to pornography in every community I have visited over the past several years. I am not talking about inactive Catholic men, but the men who take their families to Mass every Sunday. Except for parishes with less than a dozen families, it would be safe to say that there are Catholic men involved with pornography in every parish in North America. This is a monumental problem that has invaded the hearts of men in the Church. It is not going to disappear on its own. Action desperately needs to be taken at the parish level.

Prayer for Forgiveness

King David, the man after God's own heart, fell into the sin of adultery. This is his prayer to God for forgiveness: "Have mercy on me, O God, according to thy steadfast love; according to thy abundant mercy blot out my transgressions. Wash me thoroughly from my iniquity, and cleanse me from my sin!" - Psalm 51:1-2

David trusted in the steadfast love and abundant mercy of God as the source of his forgiveness. We should do the same. We should never hesitate to seek Christ's mercy in the Sacrament of Penance.

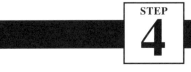

Find an Accountability Friend

Small pornography recovery and accountability groups need to be started under the direction of parish priests. Establishing accountability groups is a perfect opportunity for Catholic men's groups to cooperate with local priests and parishes in meeting one of the most critical needs of contemporary men.

Find at least one accountability friend whom you can call on 24 hours a day if needed. The telephone can help you avoid temptation at vulnerable moments. This telephone strategy is similar to Alcoholics Anonymous, where a person tempted to return to alcoholism can call on a friend anytime for prayer and encouragement. It may also be helpful to have a daily (or even a morning and evening) checkup call from your accountability friend. At a minimum, your friend should ask you every week if you have kept yourself free from sexual sin. This accountability is invaluable in helping you get through times of temptation.

If you use a computer, then "Accountability Software" should be installed (see resource section).

Douglas Weiss, himself a recovered sex addict and a nationally-known lecturer on sexual addiction, has stated, "I have not experienced, nor have I met anyone who has experienced sexual addiction recovery *alone*" [emphasis mine]. Don't be tempted to skip steps 3 and 4. You need the help of others to have a realistic hope of breaking your addiction.

"And though a man might prevail against one who is alone, two will withstand him. A threefold cord is not quickly broken." - Ecclesiastes 4:12

STEP

5

Begin a Life of Daily Scripture Reading

There isn't a quick and easy way to erase pornography from your mind. It took just a few clicks to get into it, but it will take mental discipline to get out. One cause for the extreme difficulty in erasing pornographic images from the mind is that when a man views pornography, a chemical called epinephrine is released in the brain. This release of epinephrine causes a deep imprint of the visual image to be stored within the brain. When an act of self-stimulation accompanies the pornography viewing, an even stronger release of epinephrine occurs, thus making the imprint of the image even stronger. Such images can plague a man for decades. Rest assured, there is a way out of pornography addiction – but don't fall for the promise of an easy way out.

One of the few effective means of getting these pornographic images out of your head is spending time reading and memorizing Scripture every day. For many of you it might be particularly helpful if you have a Scripture time both morning and evening. In addition, you need to begin a program of memorizing Scripture. In my experience, a disciplined plan to memorize Scripture is necessary to clear the rot out of your brain.

"Occupy your minds with good thoughts, or the enemy will fill them with bad ones. Unoccupied, they cannot be." – St. Thomas More (Source: *Voice of the Saints* by Francis W. Johnston, TAN Books, Rockford, IL 1986, p.67)

Get a copy of the two Pure Mind Scripture Memory Kits (see page 46) – and use them diligently. Scripture can supernaturally transform your mind. This is not a theory, it really works!

"For the word of God is living and active, sharper than any two-edged sword, piercing to the division of soul and spirit, of joints and marrow, and discerning the thoughts and intentions of the heart." - Hebrews 4:12

Be aware that things might appear to get worse when you begin an extensive exposure to Scripture. As the Word of God, coupled with the power of the Holy Spirit, is cutting out deeply implanted pornographic images, these very subconscious images will surface in your mind. When this happens you are in the initial stages of being cleansed from the inside out.

"For he is like a refiner's fire and like fullers' soap; he will sit as a refiner and purifier of silver, and he will purify the sons of Levi and refine them like gold and silver..." - Malachi 3:2-3

Once the rooted-out images float to your consciousness, don't dare to mentally delight in them. Pray at that instant, and use your mental discipline to put them out of your conscious thoughts. Be sure to pray for protection so that these images do not return.

Finally, put your focus on Christ – not on your problems. The most successful drug, alcohol, and pornography addiction recovery programs are those which incorporate a vital faith component. It is extremely difficult to overcome an addiction by a compulsive focus on the problem itself. The addictive appetites need to be redirected to the One who can fulfill our desires with good things (Psalm 103:5).

"It is impossible for any created good to constitute man's happiness. For happiness is the perfect good, which lulls the appetite altogether ... Now the object of the will, i.e. of man's appetite, is the universal good ... Hence it is evident that naught can lull man's will, save the universal good. This is to be found, not in any creature, but in God alone." — St. Thomas Aquinas, *Summa Theologiae*, 1-2, Question 2, Article 8

"The desire for God is written in the human heart ... Only in God will he find the truth and happiness he never stops searching for." –*Catechism of the Catholic Church* (CCC), Section 27.

"Our hearts are restless until they rest in you." – St. Augustine

Reading, meditating on, and memorizing Scripture will assist you in redirecting and transforming both your thoughts and appetites.

STEP
6

Learn to Discern & Combat Spiritual Attacks

Sexual addictions and pornography open a person up to the influence of evil spirits. Before a spiritual attack begins you may be struggling with your own lustful thoughts. A spiritual attack begins when a spirit silently intrudes into your mind, adding intensity to your lustful thoughts, or implanting additional ones. You can detect this happening when an ordinary human lust arises and then suddenly erupts into a life of its own, one that seems nearly impossible to shake.

If an episode of overwhelming lustful thoughts involves a spiritual attack, you will not be able to shake it with just mental effort alone. It is very easy to get discouraged and feel completely overwhelmed by both lust and the accompanying spiritual assault. Yet you can quickly break the power of the attack by first realizing what is happening, and then by saying a prayer for spiritual protection to your guardian angel and St. Michael the Archangel.

One of the hardest parts in fending off a spiritual attack is learning to recognize when one is happening. Spiritual attacks are covert operations that need to disguise themselves to be successful. Ask God to give you continual discernment. After a spiritual attack is stopped, your mental disciplines will still be needed to control your thoughts.

Trusting God as Your Guardian

"Oh guard my life, and deliver me; let me not be put to shame, for I take refuge in thee. May integrity and uprightness preserve me, for I wait for thee."
- Psalm 25:20-21

Wait upon God for strength. Trust in God's power to guard and uphold you.

You Need Grace — Lots of It

The Sacraments, especially the Eucharist, are like rivers of living water that bring fresh strength to your soul. Take advantage of every opportunity to receive grace by frequenting the Sacraments.

Also, use sacramentals such as holy water, crucifixes, St. Benedict medals (blessed by a priest with the exorcism prayer), etc. These can be very effective in overcoming or preventing spiritual attacks.

If your work requires travel, then you know about the additional temptations men face while on the road. I recommend wearing a crucifix or a holy medal during your entire trip, and a liberal use of holy water in your hotel room. Also, have friends praying for you on your trip. Have a friend to be accountable to upon your return.

STEP

8

Both Vices & Virtues are Strengthened by Practice

An addiction to pornography is never static. It starts with what seems like just a little dabbling in digital lusts. Before you know it you are hooked on the technological temptations. Next you begin searching for more graphic pornography. As your conscience becomes desensitized, the images that were disgusting when you started viewing pornography become enticing. The most dangerous step (one often fatal to marriage and family life) is when men want to start acting out the images they have seen.

"The alternative is clear: either man governs his passions and finds peace, or he lets himself be dominated by them and becomes unhappy." - CCC, Section 2339

If you are viewing pornography, then your vices have been strengthened by repeated practice, and the corresponding virtues of chastity and purity are very weak. It will take time, but the more you practice virtue the easier it will become. Changes resulting from the practice of virtue will give you hope and the strength to persevere.

St. Paul said, "We do not lose heart ... our inner man is being renewed day by day" (2 Corinthians 4:16). The more completely you break with your sexual addiction, the easier it will be to overcome it. Do realize, however, that it will take time, perseverance, and effort.

"For just as you once yielded your members to impurity and to greater and greater iniquity, so now yield your members to righteousness for sanctification." - Romans 6:19

Pray

Pray the Rosary often. In God's plan, the Blessed Mother is going to crush the serpent's head. Mary can play a vital role by neutralizing the serpent's venom of pornography.

St. Joseph, the guardian of the Holy Family and the protector of the Church, can powerfully assist you in the battle against sexual addiction. St. Joseph, the just and righteous man, is the perfect model of purity for men. Every Christian man struggling with pornography should ask for St. Joseph's protection and his intercession for purity.

"The prayer of a righteous man has great power in its effects." - James 5:16

Don't let the enemies of your soul keep you isolated. Ask for protection and strength from the intercessions of the saints. Ask for the intercession of your patron saint. In particular, St. Benedict's intercession is known to be exceptionally powerful against wicked spirits.

Another wise step is to contact a contemplative religious order, and ask them to pray for you daily in their intentions (cf. James 5:16). Remarkable answers to prayer result from the intercessions of a holy religious order.

Practical Physical Precautions

Your spiritual defenses are weakened when you allow yourself to become run down from too little sleep, or too much work and stress. If you are fatigued, then take extra precautions against temptations until you restore your physical condition.

Too much alcohol or the use of drugs will dull your conscience and diminish your ability to make good judgments.

"Be sober, be watchful. Your adversary the devil prowls around like a roaring lion, seeking some one to devour." - 1 Peter 5:8

Too much idle time and lots of time alone make a struggle against pornography more difficult. Fill idle time with wholesome service and other activities. You might need to make other prudent changes in order to reduce the amount of time you are alone.

As previously mentioned, pornography viewing releases chemicals in the brain that condition the mind to engage in repeated behavior so as to receive additional pleasurable stimulation. One sexual addiction therapist has experienced success with a simple exercise to help recondition the brain. The plan is to wear a rubber band on the wrist for 30 days. Every time an impure thought occurs the man snaps the rubber band, sending a neurological pain signal. Your brain is partially reconditioned as it begins to associate pain with impure thoughts.

Don't Give Up
After a Setback

An overwhelming wave of guilt and discouragement can follow in the wake of a setback. If you do fall into a sinful setback you need to be prepared for an onslaught of condemnation. The Bible calls Satan "the accuser" of Christians (Rev 12:10). After a setback Satan will be ready to bombard you with doubts of God's love for you.

St. Paul says to take "the shield of faith, with which you can quench all the flaming darts of the evil one" (Ephesians 6:16). At this point you need to call to mind those Scripture verses of God's steadfast love and mercy which you have memorized. Such verses can preserve you from condemnation and despair. (See the verses in the Pure Mind Scripture Memory Kits, and read Psalm 51 and Romans 8:31-39.)

You need to carefully discern between condemnation and conviction. Condemnation from "the accuser" has the effect of driving you away from God. Conviction from the Holy Spirit drives you towards God to find forgiveness and restoration. If you fall, you should certainly not give up the fight. Get to the Sacrament of Penance and ask for God's forgiveness. It will always be there for you.

"If the Lord delights in a man's way, he makes his steps firm; though he stumble, he will not fall, for the Lord upholds him with his hand." - Psalm 37:23-24

STEP 12

Ask Your Wife for Assistance

Your wife probably knows about your addiction already and is emotionally crushed by it. You are probably only fooling yourself by lying to your wife about your pornography addiction. Stop lying to her about it.

Lying to your wife about where you have been, where money has been spent, or denials about pornographic usage destroys trust and further weakens your marriage. Many wives find the lying about pornography as devastating as the addiction itself. You need your wife's patience, prayers, and perseverance in helping you overcome this addiction. Lying can destroy your marriage. Stop the lying and speak the truth to her, no matter how humbling it may be. Most wives are willing to help their husbands overcome an addiction – if their husbands are honest with them. A humble and honest husband will discover a valuable ally in overcoming pornography (See Ecclesiastes 4:12).

Stop blame-shifting – it is one of the world's oldest ways of avoiding moral responsibility. [Remember the lame excuse that Adam gave God for eating the forbidden fruit (Genesis 3)?] Your pornography addiction is not your wife's fault. It is the result of your sinful moral choices. The road to repentance and recovery begins when you assume responsibility for your actions.

Although men are often reluctant to do so, it would be wise to communicate your sexual needs in a gentle way to your wife. St. Thomas Aquinas when discussing the mutual obligation for payment of the marriage debt says, "Marriage is directed to the avoiding of fornication" (1 Corinthians 7:2). He mentions that this precept about the mutual obligation regarding the marriage debt is particularly important when a spouse is troubled by concupiscence. (See *Summa Theologica*, Supplement Question 64 at www.newadvent.org/summa/506400.htm.)

"Do not refuse one another except perhaps by agreement for a season, that you may devote yourselves to prayer; but then come together again, lest Satan tempt you through lack of self-control." - 1 Corinthians 7:5

"Let your fountain be blessed, and rejoice in the wife of your youth, a lovely hind, a graceful doe. Let her affection fill you at all times with delight, be infatuated always with her love. Why should you be infatuated, my son, with a loose woman and embrace the bosom of an adventuress?" - Proverbs 5:18-20

In all likelihood, you have harmed your marriage during the course of your pornographic addiction. Weakened marital communication, trust, intimacy, and sexual relations frequently accompany addiction to pornography. Take steps now to strengthen your marriage.

For a list of available organizations and practical ways to strengthen your marriage go to www.dads.org and scroll down to click on "Links," and then click on "Help for Hurting Marriages."

As you wean yourself from pornography your marriage life will improve. Likewise, strengthening your marriage will fortify you against the lure of pornography.

APPPENDIX

Scripture Memory
for a Pure Mind

*A man serious about keeping, or restoring,
purity will meditate on God's Word regularly:
"How can a young man keep his way pure?
By guarding it according to thy word." - Psalm 119:9*

Romans 12:2

"Do not be conformed to this world but be transformed by the renewal of your mind, that you may prove what is the will of God, what is good and acceptable and perfect."

Comment: A vital part of a life transformation is renewing your mind. The Scriptures, coupled with the power of the Holy Spirit, have the ability to renew your mind from deep within. These internal changes eventually result in an outwardly transformed life.

James 1:14-15

"But each person is tempted when he is lured and enticed by his own desire. Then desire when it has conceived gives birth to sin; and sin when it is full-grown brings forth death."

Comment: There is a process in the growth of sin. It starts with a willful delight in an enticement to sinful desires. Without resistance on our part, the progress towards sin is never halted. The next step is consenting to and yielding to the temptation in a sinful act. With the sin of viewing pornography there is the commission of a gravely sinful act. For many, the addiction to pornography leads to a desire to commit many of the perverted acts viewed. The wisest way to stop this dreadful process is to resist the very first temptation to sin.

1 Peter 5:8-9

"Be sober, be watchful. Your adversary the devil prowls around like a roaring lion, seeking some one to devour. Resist him, firm in your faith, knowing that the same experience of suffering is required of your brotherhood throughout the world."

Comment: Watch and be on your guard for temptation. Remember the devil often tempts at moments we might not expect, during times of stress, and when we are sick or exhausted. You must firmly resist a spiritual attack with prayer, use of sacramentals, and by recalling to mind words of Scripture.

Galatians 6:7-8

"Do not be deceived; God is not mocked, for whatever a man sows, that he will also reap. For he who sows to his own flesh will from the flesh reap corruption; but he who sows to the Spirit will from the Spirit reap eternal life."

Comment: Don't be misled by those who say "pornography is no big deal." Sins, like pornography, have predictable consequences. Sowing pornography into your mind will harm your marriage and corrupt your spiritual life. Sowing good things in your mind and heart will result in spiritual growth and eternal life.

Proverbs 5:3-5, 8

"For the lips of a loose woman drip honey, and her speech is smoother than oil, but in the end she is bitter as wormwood, sharp as a two-edged sword. Her feet go down to death; her steps follow the path to Sheol...Keep your way far from her, and do not go near the door of her house."

Comment: Proverbs warns about the flattering and seductive speech of the loose woman. Remember that her "sweet" sounding words are really poison. The wisest way to keep yourself from problems with other women is to avoid going anywhere near places where you know temptation exists.

Psalm 101:3-4

"I will not set before my eyes anything that is base. I hate the work of those who fall away; it shall not cleave to me. Perverseness of heart shall be far from me; I will know nothing of evil."

Comment: Memorize and internalize these verses. Be determined to make them your standard. It might be wise to place these verses on your computer monitor and on top of your TV.

Sirach 21:2

"Flee from sin as from a snake; for if you approach sin, it will bite you. Its teeth are lion's teeth, and destroy the souls of men."

Comment: Pornography is like the venom of a cobra. Flee from it. Those foolish enough to toy with it risk destroying their souls.

Psalm 51:10

"Create in me a clean heart, O God, and put a new and right spirit within me."

Comment: This is King David's prayer asking God to cleanse and renew his heart. God can restore men who have fallen into serious sin. This verse can be wisely used as a daily prayer.

Ephesians 4:22-24

"Put off your old nature which belongs to your former manner of life and is corrupt through deceitful lusts, and be renewed in the spirit of your minds, and put on the new nature, created after the likeness of God in true righteousness and holiness."

Comment: If you really want to live a new life in Christ, then you must quit filling your mind with deceitful lusts. Christ can help you renew your mind, but you must "put off" the corrupt lifestyle.

Philippians 4:8

"Finally, brethren, whatever is true, whatever is honorable, whatever is just, whatever is pure, whatever is lovely, whatever is gracious, if there is any excellence, if there is anything worthy of praise, think about these things."

Comment: You can't fight something with nothing. You can't fight old pornographic images in your mind without having a positive replacement for them.

Sirach 7:36

"In all you do, remember the end of your life, and then you will never sin."

Comment: When tempted to sin, just picture yourself standing before the judgment seat of Christ. Such a sobering focus on the end of your life will help keep you from sin.

Hebrews 4:12

"For the Word of God is living and active, sharper than any two-edged sword, piercing to the division of soul and spirit, of joints and marrow, and discerning the thoughts and intentions of the heart."

Comment: What can cut out the pornographic images implanted deep within your memory? The Word of God has unparalleled power to cleanse you, even in the deepest part of your mind.

ONLINE RESOURCES

There is a continual need for updated lists of resources and helpful new ministries. At the time of publication, there is not yet a national Catholic organization with the primary mission of assisting men seeking freedom from pornography addiction. Our web site will post updates when these outreaches are available.

To see a current listing of resources and organizations: go to www.dads.org > Click on links > Click on Help for Those Struggling with Pornography.

Freedom TeleGroups for Men
www.bravehearts.net
TeleGroups offer a safe and anonymous place for men struggling with sexual purity. Men receive support and encouragement from the honest and transparent dialog. Using the "L.I.F.E. Guide," they are equipped with effective strategies to overcome

sexual addictions. This is a non-denominational Christian outreach. Hopefully, there will be Catholic small TeleGroups started in the near future. Email info@bravehearts.net.

Helpline for Pornography Addiction
1-800-583-2964 - www.nationalcoalition.org

Trained counselors are available during business hours to help individuals addicted to pornography. Assistance is offered to the spouses of those addicted. Sponsored by the National Coalition for the Protection of Children and Families.

Computer Programs for Sexual Purity
www.we-blocker.com

We-Blocker Internet filtering software. Free download of program and free updates. Have your spouse, or friend, maintain the We-Blocker password on the computers you use.

www.xxxchurch.com

X3 Watch is a free accountability software program offered by XXXchurch.com (other organizations charge as much as $20 per month for this service). Whenever you visit a questionable site, X3 Watch saves the site name on your computer. Every 2 weeks your accountability partner will receive an email containing the questionable sites you may have visited. This report only goes to your chosen accountability partner and is not stored or used by XXXchurch.com or any other organization.

Internet Resources & Organizations Dealing with Pornography
www.pureintimacy.org
A website for those struggling to overcome online pornography, as well as spouses of those struggling, sponsored by Focus on the Family.

www.sexaa.org
Sex Addicts Anonymous (SAA) has group meetings throughout North America that follow the AA 12-step model. This and other 12-step groups vary in quality, depending upon leadership and make-up of the local group. Discernment is required.

www.sa.org
Sexaholics Anonymous (SA) has group meetings throughout the world that follow the 12-step model. Quality of local chapters vary. Careful discernment is required in evaluating a local group.

RESOURCES

Breaking Free: 12 Steps to Sexual Purity - Tape Album
This 3-tape series offers practical assistance to help prevent and overcome an addiction to pornography. On tape one, Steve Wood outlines twelve steps to sexual purity for men. On tape two, Steve Wood interviews Laurie Hall (author, *An Affair of the Mind*) as she shares the devastating effects of pornography on a family and how to save a marriage after a pornography addiction. Tape three is a riveting interview with Steve Wood and Scott Hahn on the healing power of confession. *3 tape album* $19.95

Pure Mind Scripture Memory Kits
These are invaluable resources for men struggling to find freedom from pornography. Each card has a different Bible verse you can memorize for a pure mind. They can fit in your pocket so they are always at your fingertips. 20 cards in each kit. Volume I: $3.95, Volume II: $3.95

Lord, Have Mercy: The Healing Power of Confession
This book by Scott Hahn is a terrific guide to help understand the healing power of the Sacrament of Penance. Hardcover, $19.95

A Contemporary Adult Guide to Conscience for the Sacrament of Confession
An invaluable booklet for making a good confession. Includes an examination of conscience. $2.95

FREE Pure Mind Scripture Program

This is an invaluable resource for anyone desiring sexual purity. It is available for free download from www.dads.org > resources > Pornography > Pure Mind Scripture Program. A different scripture verse will appear each time the computer starts up. Recommended by confessors and spiritual advisors.

FREE Electronic Newsletter for Men

St. Joseph's Covenant Keepers offers a FREE electronic monthly newsletter that encourages men to become godly husbands and fathers. Short, concise, and straight-to-the-point, it offers practical assitance to help men become the best husbands and dads they can be. Sign up at www.dads.org.

Multiple Copies of this Booklet

1 Copy: $2.95
10 Copies: $2.00/ea.   ($20)
50 Copies: $1.50/ea.   ($75)
100 Copies: $1.25/ea.   ($125)
500 Copies: $1.00/ea.   ($500)
1000 Copies: $0.75/ea. ($750)

(Special pricing available for priests distributing these booklets in the confessional)

All resources are available from the Family Life Center
22226 Westchester Blvd. - Port Charlotte, FL 33952
www.dads.org or **(800) 705-6131**

ABOUT THE AUTHOR

Steve Wood has led youth, campus, and pro-life ministries. A graduate of Gordon-Conwell Theological Seminary, he served as an Evangelical pastor for a decade before converting to Catholicism. He started the Family Life Center International in 1992. Steve is also the founder of St. Joseph's Covenant Keepers, a movement that seeks to transform society through the transformation of fathers and families. Utilizing his book *Christian Fatherhood*, audio and video tapes, television, radio and conferences, Steve has reached tens of thousands of men in the USA, Canada and overseas with a message of Christian faith and responsibility. He is the host of the live *Faith and Family* broadcasts on EWTN worldwide radio (www.ewtn.com), as well as the host of *The Carpenter Shop*, a television show for fathers on EWTN. A member of the American Counseling Association, Steve is also a Certified Family Life Educator. In addition, he is a professional Christian Life Coach with a private practice (www.halftimecoaching.com) for those seeking to refine and refocus life mission, purpose, and priorities and to develop strategies for achieving life goals.

Steve and his wife Karen have been married twenty-five years and are the parents of eight children.